The Financ   Kid's (

A Mini-Mogul's Introduction to the Stock Market

An introduction to stock investing, a great way for kids and their parents to learn investing together!

Savvy Books Publishing

Copyright © 2023 by Savvy Books Publishing

All rights reserved. No part of this book may be used or reproduced by any means, graphic, electronic, or mechanical, including photocopying, recording, taping, or by any information storage retrieval system, without the written permission of the publisher except in the case of brief quotations embodied in critical articles and reviews.

Table of Contents

Note to Parents, ... 2

Introduction 3

Chapter 1 9

What is the Stock Market 9

    What is a Company 9

    Finding Stock Prices: 15

Chapter 2: 21

Investing in the Stock Market 21

    Value Investing and Fundamental Analysis .. 28

    Technical Analysis 28

    Contrarian Thinking and Investing 29

    Stock Market Strategies: The Art of Trading Over Time 30

Chapter 3 35

The Magic of Investing in Various Funds and other Investments - A Grandparent's Tale 35

    Index Funds: The Colorful Palette of Investing 38

Why Use Diversification? 40

Bond Funds: A Smooth Sail in the World of Investing 40

Options: Like a Coupon for Stocks! 45

Attention Parents: 48

Mid-Book Review Request 48

Economics and Economies 51

Why Economies Matter to Us 53

The World Economies and the Stock Market: A Global Game of Business 55

Chapter 4: 59

Putting your new Knowledge to Work! 59

Why Diverse Investments Matter 65

The Role of the Economy in the Stock Market 67

Economic Indicators: Clues to the Economy's Health 68

Start Small and Learn 70

The Importance of Research 71

A Final Note to Parents: Nurturing Financial Literacy in Your Child..79

A Note of Thanks 83

Keeping the Game Alive 83

References: 88

Note to Parents,

This book will serve as a great introduction to the stock market for your child. While learning about investing can be complex and challenging, understanding the stock market's basics is essential to your child's education.

This book is designed to teach your child about the mechanics of the stock market and financial literacy, critical thinking, and general knowledge about the world around them. By reading this book together, you and your child will have meaningful discussions about money, economics, and the world of finance.

Thank you for choosing this book as a valuable resource for your child's education and financial future.

Introduction

Alright Kids, here we go!

Money has been used to buy and sell things for a long time. Sometimes, the things we want are expensive, and saving enough money to buy them can be challenging. But have you ever heard of a way to make your money grow faster than you can save it? It's called investing, and it's like planting a money seed that can grow into a big money tree! Investing means putting your money into something that has the potential to make more money over time, like stocks. Stocks are like tiny pieces of a company that you can buy and sell, and as the company does well, your stock can become more valuable. It's like a game, but with money!

Now, investing isn't just for grown-ups - kids can do it too! Of course, you'll need some help from your parents, but once you understand the basics, investing can be a fun and exciting way to learn about money and how it works. Here are some of the things you'll learn as you dive into the world of investing:

- How to research companies and figure out which ones might be good investments.
- The different types of stocks and other investments out there.
- The importance of diversifying your investments (basically, not putting all your eggs in one basket).

Investing is a powerful tool for building financial security and learning about business and finance. By understanding the basics of investing as a kid, you'll be well-prepared to make intelligent financial decisions. So, strap on your money belt and get ready to ride the stock market rollercoaster! It's going to be a wild and educational ride.

Benjamin was a curious 12-year-old living in New Jersey, just outside New York City. One day, as he was watching T.V. with his Dad, a news report caught his attention: the Dow Jones Industrial Average had reached a new high.

Benjamin: *"Dad, what's the stock market? I keep hearing about it on the news."*

Dad: *"Ah, the stock market! Well, it's like a giant marketplace for buying and selling pieces of companies. Imagine if you could own a tiny piece of your favorite company - like Apple, Disney, or Nike - and as the company grows and makes money, your piece becomes more valuable. That's the stock market!"*

Benjamin: *"So, the more popular the company, the more valuable the stock?"*

Dad*: "That's right! When the news says the Dow Jones Industrial Average has reached a new high, the value of the stocks of the biggest companies in*

America is increasing. It's like the whole marketplace is celebrating success!"

Benjamin's mind was racing with excitement. The idea of owning a piece of his favorite companies was thrilling! He imagined his stocks growing and growing like magic beans in a fairytale. He bombarded his Dad with questions, wanting to know more about how the stock market worked and how he could get involved. His Dad laughed and said, 'Slow down, kiddo! We'll learn more about the stock market together, but let's start with the basics first.

Fun Facts about Kids' Stock Market Success!

Advait Arya:

At 16, Advait Arya, a student in Abu Dhabi, began trading in the stock market with Dh 8,000 (eight thousand dirhams is worth USD 2,178.28), which he saved over four to five years. He learned the fundamentals of trading from his father and online resources like Investopedia and YouTube. Advait has made safe, long-term investments in major companies and plans to take a gap year after Grade 12 to be more active in the stock market. Since starting his journey in the stock market, he has experienced significant success. He more than triple his initial investment of Dh8,000 ($2,178.28), growing it to Dh30,000 ($8,168.49) within a year. Advait focused on making safe, long-term investments in major companies like Amazon, Apple, Google, and Facebook. Additionally, he invested in the U.S. video game company Electronic Arts, citing its potential to revolutionize the video game industry. His strategic and cautious approach to avoiding volatile companies was crucial to his successful investment outcomes. (1)

Chapter 1
What is the Stock Market

What is a Company

A Company is like a team working together towards a common goal, like a sports team or a group of superheroes. Each person in the company has a different role, and together, they make the company successful. For example, the CEO is like the team captain, the marketing department is like the cheerleaders, and the finance team is like the accountants. But, unlike a sports team or a group of superheroes, a company is a legal entity, which means it has certain rights and responsibilities under the law. (2)(6)

Imagine a world where shoes can fly, princesses can slay dragons, and superhero battles can occur in outer space! Welcome to the world of companies like Nike, Disney, and Apple.

With its signature swoosh logo and catchy slogan, "Just Do It," Nike creates sneakers, clothing, and gear that help athletes of all levels perform at their best. Whether on the basketball court or the track, Nike's gear helps athletes push the limits of what they thought was possible.

Disney is the mastermind behind some of the world's most beloved movies, T.V. shows, and theme parks. From the magical kingdoms of Cinderella and Aladdin to the intergalactic battles of Star Wars and the superhero antics of the Marvel universe, Disney creates stories that capture the imagination and inspire wonder in people of all ages. Finally, there's Apple, the company that revolutionized technology use.

These companies can create amazing products and services because they are successful businesses. They have employees who work hard daily to bring their products to life. They use profits from selling their products to invest in new technologies and ideas and to hire more people to help them grow. They also advertise and market their products to customers worldwide, which helps spread the word about their work. This is possible because they are structured as companies with a clear vision, a robust business model, and a commitment to excellence.

What is a Publicly Traded Company, and How is it Different from a Private Company

Owning a piece of your favorite company - a video game, a toy company, or a sports team - is like owning a pizza slice! That's what owning shares of stock is like. Each share represents a tiny piece of ownership in a company, and the more shares you own, the more ownership you have. When the company does well, the value of your shares goes up, and when the company struggles, the value of your shares goes down. It's like being a part of the team - when the team wins, you win, and when the team loses, you lose. But owning shares of stock is even better than owning a slice of pizza because the company can keep growing and getting better over time, making your slice of the pie bigger and better, too!

A public company as a big, bustling restaurant, where anyone can walk in and buy a share of the business. That's right - anyone can become a part owner of a public company just by purchasing shares of its stock. This means that the company's ownership is spread out among many people, and no one person or group has total control. This is different from a private company, which is like a small, exclusive club where only a select few people are invited to be members. Private companies aren't open to the general public, and their shares aren't available for purchase on the stock market. Public companies are like open-door restaurants, and private companies are like private clubs.(3)(7)

Here are some more public companies you may know:
- Nintendo (the gaming company that created Mario, Zelda, and Pokémon!)
- Hasbro (the masterminds behind Monopoly, Nerf, and My Little Pony!)

- Nike (the athletic brand that sponsors some of the world's most famous athletes!)
- Disney (the entertainment giant behind everything from classic animated movies to blockbuster Marvel films!)

Can you think of any others? If your favorite company is a public company, you can buy shares in it. Look it up and find out!

Owning shares in a successful business can pay off with big bucks!

Here are the main ways a shareholder can make money:

- Capital gains: When a company's stock price goes up, the shareholder's shares are worth more. If the shareholder sells the shares at a higher price than they bought them for, they make a profit, called a "capital gain."
- Dividends: Some companies pay their shareholders regular cash payments called dividends. It's like getting a little

thank-you check for being an owner of the company.
- Stock splits: Sometimes, a company will decide to increase the number of shares outstanding, which can increase the value of the shares. It's like cutting a pizza into more slices, but each is still the same size!

Finding Stock Prices:

Many people turn to a ticker tape to keep tabs on stock prices - a scrolling display of real-time stock prices on financial news channels. The ticker tape displays the ticker symbol (a unique, abbreviated code for each stock) and the current price of each stock. The price is constantly updated, sometimes as often as every few seconds, to provide the most recent information. By keeping an eye on the ticker tape, you can quickly see how the overall market is performing and how specific stocks are doing. Common ticker symbols for the companies mentioned above are Nintendo (NTDOY), Nike (NKE), and Hasbro (HAS).

What are Stock Markets, and Where are They?

1611, the **Amsterdam Stock Exchange** became the first modern stock trading market. This revolutionized how businesses were able to raise capital and gain funding. The **Dutch East India Company** was the first publicly traded company, and by selling stock and paying dividends on shares to investors, it opened the door to the creation of stock exchanges worldwide. The idea quickly spread to other countries, and today, the major stock markets include the New York Stock Exchange (NYSE), the Nasdaq, the Tokyo Stock Exchange (TSE), and the London Stock Exchange (LSE). (1)

The global stock market is a complex network of interconnected exchanges, each with its unique focus. For example, the New York Stock Exchange, or NYSE, is home to many of the largest companies in the world, including tech giants like Apple and Amazon. Meanwhile, the Nasdaq, also located in New York City, is known for its focus on tech companies like Facebook, Google, and Tesla. Over in Japan, the Tokyo Stock Exchange is a central hub for Asian companies, with Toyota, Sony, and Nintendo all trading on the exchange. These are just a few examples of the many exchanges that make up the dynamic and ever-changing landscape of the global stock market. (1)(2)(3)(4)(5)

(Stock Brokers) Who Assists Buyers and Sellers?

A stockbroker is a person who helps investors buy and sell shares of companies on the stock market. They work for brokerage firms and provide advice, research, and guidance to their clients about which stocks to buy or sell. Stockbrokers are also responsible for executing trades (Buying or Selling) on behalf of their clients, meaning they place the buy and sell orders in the market. They are compensated through commissions, which are a percentage of the total value of the trade. Think of them like a personal shopper for stocks - they help you find the best "deals" in the market and make sure the transaction goes smoothly.

Bulls and Bears

Once upon a time, in the wild and wooly days of the 18th century a strange new language emerged in finance. People began to use the terms "bull" and "bear" to describe how the stock market was doing. Some say it came from how the animal's attacked - bulls thrusting their horns up, like stocks going up, and bears swiping down, like stocks going down. Others think it's because "bull" sounds like "boom" and "bear" sounds like "bust" - just like the economy! No one knows for sure, but these terms have stuck around for centuries, and they're still used to describe stock market conditions today. It's like a secret code language for finance geeks. (6) When the price is going up, it is called Bullish, and when it goes down it is called Bearish.

How Do Companies Become Public Companies?

An Initial Public Offering, or IPO, is a special event where a company sells shares to the public for the first time. The company gets to raise money and become a publicly traded company. The public can invest in the company and profit from it. It's like a big ol' party with cake and investing. (7)

Everything in a Nutshell

Stocks, shares, stock exchanges, bulls and bears, and IPOs - it's a lot to take in, but together, they make up the exciting world of investing. Stocks are like pieces of a company that people can buy and sell, shares are individual pieces of stock, stock exchanges are where they're bought and sold, and bulls and bears are terms for how the market is doing. IPOs are the big event where a company goes public and offers its shares to everyone.

Investing can be a game, with ups and downs and opportunities to win big.

Fun Facts about Kids' Stock Market Success!

Warren Buffett: *Warren Buffett (Known as the "Oracle of Omaha,") bought his first stock at 11. He purchased three shares of Cities Service Preferred at $38 per share. Although the stock initially fell to $27, Buffett held on until it reached $40, before selling. Unfortunately, the stock later skyrocketed to nearly $200 a share, teaching him a valuable lesson about patience in investing.*

Chapter 2: Investing in the Stock Market

Benjamin's Dad brings him to meet the Financial Planner, Mr. Smith:

"As a financial planner, my job is to help people make smart decisions about their money. I work with all kinds of people, from families to businesses to retirees, and my goal is to help them create a financial plan that works for them. It's like being a personal coach for money - I help people understand their finances, set goals, and create a plan to achieve them. I use my experience and knowledge to help clients make informed decisions about investing, saving, and budgeting. It's a gratifying job because I get to see my clients reach their financial goals and know that I played a part in helping them get there."

Famous Investors:

Benjamin Graham (1894-1976): He was like a superhero of investing, with a mission to help people make intelligent decisions about their money. Born in England, his family moved to New York City when he was just a baby and became a bright guy with a degree from Columbia University. Benjamin worked on Wall Street and even started his own investment in honest and transparent companies that gave shareholders a fair share of their profits was one of his core beliefs. He believed in investing in honest and transparent companies that gave shareholders a fair share of their profits. He was a champion for investors and fought against corporations trying to hide their financial state. He pioneered the investing world, and his ideas have influenced generations of investors. He may not have worn a cape or had superpowers, but his impact on the financial world was heroic!

Warren Buffett (1930-)is a legendary investor, often called the "Oracle of Omaha."

Like a wise wizard, he has made a fortune through investing in stocks and companies, using his keen eye for value and his patient, disciplined approach. He started investing when he was just a kid, and today, his investments are worth billions of dollars. His success is a testament to his dedication, hard work, and unique investing approach. Buffett is known for his "value investing" style, which focuses on finding undervalued companies and buying them up at a bargain. He's like a bargain hunter but for stocks and companies! He's also known for his humility and belief in the power of self-development. He once said, "The best investment you can make is in yourself," and that's certainly true in his case. Warren Buffett is a true inspiration for anyone who wants to make it big in investing!

One of Warren's most well-known accomplishments is with Berkshire-Hathaway; he brought it from a failing business to a financial powerhouse. Warren Buffett's contributions to Berkshire Hathaway have been nothing short of remarkable. When Buffett first bought shares in the company in the 1960s, it was a struggling textile manufacturer on the brink of bankruptcy. But Buffett saw potential in the company and its leadership and set out to turn it into a powerhouse of investments.

Buffett helped transform Berkshire Hathaway into a diversified holding company with a portfolio of top-tier businesses through his expert stock-picking and business acumen. He's made shrewd acquisitions of companies like GEICO and Dairy Queen, and he's used the company's strong cash flow to make strategic investments in industries like insurance, energy, and technology.

Today, Berkshire Hathaway is one of the world's largest and most successful holding companies, thanks to Buffett's visionary leadership and investment savvy. It's safe to say that Berkshire Hathaway would be a very different company without Buffett - and the investing world would be very different!

Those who invested $10,000 in Berkshire Hathaway in 1965 are above the $165 million mark today.

Bill Ackman (1966-) is a famous investor who runs a Pershing Square Capital Management hedge fund. Like a coach helps a sports team win, Ackman helps companies grow by investing in them. He's been really successful at this. Between 2003 and 2021, he managed to increase the money in his fund by 17.1% yearly, much more than the average growth of big companies in the U.S. stock market.

Ackman secret to success is his unique way of investing. He doesn't just put money into companies; he gets involved in their decisions. By owning a big part of a company, he can suggest changes to make the company better.

This approach has helped him and the companies he invests in do really well. (6)

Carl Icahn (1936-) is another big name in the investing world, much like a champion in a long-running sports league. For many years, even decades, he's been really good at growing money, often achieving more than 10% yearly gains. This is quite impressive!

What makes Icahn special is his bold way of investing. He doesn't just buy small pieces of companies; he believes big chunks. Then, like a coach giving a team a pep talk, he actively suggests changes in these companies to make them more valuable, especially for people who own shares. This approach of getting deeply involved and pushing for improvements sets him apart and has contributed to his remarkable success.

For further insight into Carl Icahn's investment strategies and his impact on the companies he invests in, you can look into the book *"King Icahn: The Biography of a Renegade Capitalist"* by Mark Stevens. This book provides a detailed account of Icahn's career and bold financial world approaches. (7)

Different Investing Styles:

In the exciting world of finance and investing, there are different ways that investors think about and choose their investments. Let's explore some of these investment philosophies, like other game plans in sports, each with its own way of winning.

Value Investing and Fundamental Analysis

Value investing is like shopping for a great deal. Investors look for stocks that cost less than their worth, like finding a hidden treasure at a lower price. The idea is to buy these 'undervalued' stocks and sell them later when their price increases, making a profit. (1) This is based on the stock's intrinsic value, like its true worth.

Fundamental analysis is being a detective, examining different clues about a company. Investors look at the company's financial health, industry, and economy to determine if a stock is a good buy. It's a thorough way to predict if a company will grow in value over time. (2)

Technical Analysis

Technical analysis is trying to predict the future by looking at patterns from the past. Investors use charts and graphs to study how stock prices have moved and how many people have bought or sold them. They believe these patterns can tell them what might happen next with a stock's price. (3) It's like forecasting the weather by looking at past weather patterns.

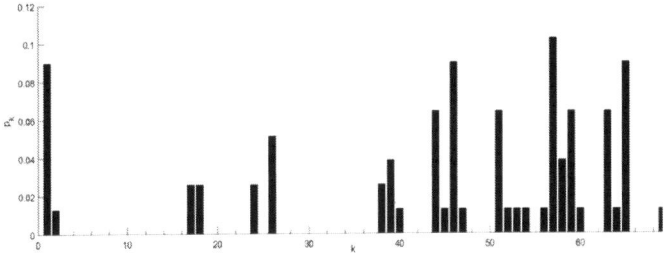

Contrarian Thinking and Investing

Contrarian thinking is about going against the crowd. In investing, contrarians do the opposite of what most people are doing. They buy stocks when others are selling and sell when others are buying, believing that the majority might only sometimes be suitable. (4) It's like choosing to run in a different direction in a game, hoping to find an advantage.

Each of these investment philosophies has its own unique approach, and understanding them can be learning different strategies in a game.

Knowing these can help make better decisions in the world of investing.

Stock Market Strategies: The Art of Trading Over Time

As we continue our journey through the exciting world of the stock market, it's time to turn our attention to different trading and investing styles. Like many ways to play a game, various approaches exist to buy and sell stocks. This section will explore three main styles: day trading, swing trading, and long-term investing. Each style has its own unique purpose, advantages, and disadvantages.

Day Trader

Imagine being a day trader, much like a sprinter in a fast-paced race. Day traders are the quick thinkers of the finance world. They buy and sell stocks or other securities all within the same day, hoping to take advantage of short-term price changes. (7) It's kind of playing a video game where you must make fast moves to win points.

For instance, if a day trader buys a company share in the morning and sells it a few hours later because the price has increased, they practice day trading. (8) This might sound exciting as it's a fast track to making money. Still, it's crucial to understand that day trading requires significant effort and skill. It's risky and usually done by experts with lots of experience and resources. (6) Even these professionals can face losses, so it's not something to jump into without careful thought.

Swing Trading

Let's imagine you're a middle-distance runner, pacing yourself between a sprint and a marathon. This is similar to swing trading in the world of finance. Swing traders hold onto their stocks or other securities for several days or weeks, aiming to earn profits over this short to medium period. (7) They're not in a rush like day traders but also not as patient as long-term investors.

Swing trading sits comfortably between the fast-paced world of day trading and the patient approach of long-term investing. It typically involves holding positions for a short to medium length of time. The profit from each trade is generally more than what you'd expect from day trading but less than from long-term investing. (5)

Long-Term Investing

Let's picture ourselves as marathon runners, steady and focused on the long journey ahead. This is akin to long-term investing in the stock market. Long-term investors, often called 'buy-and-hold' investors, buy assets like stocks and hold onto them for an extended period, typically five years or more, to maximize returns over time. (5) This approach is about patience and a belief in the growth of investments over years. Long-term investing is an excellent strategy for saving for future goals like retirement or a child's college fund. It's a favorite approach of famous investor Warren Buffett, known for his wise and patient investment choices. (9)

Wrapping Up Our Investment Journey

We have explored different investment styles, including day trading, swing trading, and long-term investing. Each style has its own pace and requires other skills. Day trading is a quick sprint where you make rapid decisions, while swing trading is a relay race where you hold onto your investments for a bit longer. Long-term investing is as a marathon, requiring patience and a long-term vision.

It's important to remember that there is no one-size-fits-all approach to investing. People have different goals, lifestyles, and levels of risk tolerance. It would help if you chose the style that suits you best.

As we end this chapter on different investment styles, we look forward to discussing the importance of diversifying your investments. Diversification is adding different flavors to your favorite meal to make it even better! You'll learn how mixing different types of investments can make your financial journey more balanced and enjoyable. So, let's turn the page and continue our adventure!

Fun Facts about Kids' and Money!

Did you know that the concept of a piggy bank, where many kids start learning about saving money, has existed for centuries? The oldest piggy banks had no holes at the bottom, so people had to break them to get the cash out. This made it a real commitment to save! Today, piggy banks are young investor's first savings account, teaching the value of saving over time. Investing, the longer you leave your money in your piggy bank, the more it grows. So, every coin you add to your piggy bank is making a small investment in your future!

Chapter 3
The Magic of Investing in Various Funds and other Investments - A Grandparent's Tale

"Benjamin, have you ever wondered how a tiny seed grows into a giant tree?" Grandpa asked, his eyes twinkling with excitement. Sitting in their cozy living room, Benjamin shook his head, curious about where this was going.

Grandma smiled and added, *"Well, we have a story to tell you about our own kind of 'magic seeds' that grew over time - it's about how we can enjoy our golden years without worry."*

Grandpa leaned forward, his voice filled with enthusiasm. *"Many years ago, we started planting our seeds in index funds. Think of them like baskets of different seeds that grow at their own pace, some fast, some slow, but all together,* they create a beautiful garden."

"And the most magical part?" Grandma chimed in, *"It's called compounding. Like a snowball rolling down a hill, picking up more snow, our money grew bigger and bigger over the years. We didn't just earn money on what*

we put in, but also on the money that our money made!"

Benjamin's eyes widened. *"So, your money was making its own money?"* he asked, *amazed.*

"Exactly, Benjamin!" Grandpa said with a nod. *"That's how we can retire comfortably and have adventures even now. And it all started with a simple decision to invest consistently for our future."*

"Wow, that's like magic!" Benjamin exclaimed, his imagination already running wild with the possibilities.

Grandma and Grandpa shared a knowing look, their hearts full of joy. They were not just sharing their journey of smart investing but planting the seeds of financial wisdom in their beloved grandson.

Let's take a look at some of the ways that Grandma and Grandpa decided to invest their money. They chose special investments called mutual funds, index funds, and bond funds.

Index Funds: The Colorful Palette of Investing

Imagine you're painting a big picture. You use many colors instead of just one color to make your painting rich and interesting. This is similar to how an index fund works in investing.

Understanding Index Funds

An index fund is like a collection of various stocks from different companies, all brought together. When you invest in an index fund, you're not just buying one stock; you're buying small parts of a whole range of stocks that belong to a market index. A market index is a group of stocks representing a stock market segment (A segment is a group of companies in the same category, such as Transportation

Companies, Food Companies, or Computer Companies).

For instance, the Vanguard 500 Index Fund includes stocks from the Standard and Poor's 500, a collection of the 500 biggest companies in the United States. (1) There's also the Nasdaq-100 Index Fund, which focuses on technology companies. By investing in these funds, you're getting a slice of different sectors of the economy.

The Power of Diversification

Diversification is a crucial concept here. It's like eating a balanced diet with different types of food. You don't just eat apples every day; you mix in oranges, bananas, and berries for variety and health benefits. In investing, diversification works similarly. You reduce the risk of losing money by spreading your investment across various stocks. If one stock doesn't do well, others might perform better, balancing your investment.

Famous investor Warren Buffett once said, "Do not put all your eggs in one basket." This quote highlights the importance of diversification in investing. (2) Its about not relying on just one stock or sector. Diversification helps manage risk and is an intelligent strategy for investors, especially if you're new to investing and want to build a stable and diversified portfolio.

Why Use Diversification?

Diversification is essential because it helps to spread out risk. The stock market can be unpredictable, and having your money spread across different types of investments can protect you from unexpected downturns in any one area. It's a way to guard your investments against big losses and is an effective method to grow your wealth steadily over time.

Bond Funds: A Smooth Sail in the World of Investing

As we navigate the exciting world of the stock market, it's important to know about a kind of investment offering a smoother ride: bond funds. These are different from buying individual stocks and can be a wise choice for young investors.

Understanding Bond Funds

Think of bond funds as a big boat carrying a variety of cargo. Instead of lending money to one entity, like with a single bond, when you invest in a bond fund, you're pooling your money with other investors to lend to various entities. This could include governments or corporations. The fund is managed by professionals who mix of bonds for the fund (4).

The Simplicity and Diversification of Bond Funds

One of the great things about bond funds is their simplicity. You don't have to pick individual bonds yourself; the fund managers do that. It's like having a captain and crew to navigate the boat for you. Also, bond funds offer diversification. This means your investment is spread out over many different bonds, reducing the risk of putting all your money in one place.

(1) Its like having various snacks in your lunchbox; if one could be better, you have other snacks.

Why Bond Funds?

Bond funds can be a wise choice for young investors because they offer a more stable and less risky investment than stocks. While they may grow slower than stock investments, they tend to provide steadier returns. This makes them an important part of a balanced investment strategy. (5)

In investing, bond funds are like a calm sea compared to the sometimes stormy ocean of the stock market. They provide a way to grow your money at a steadier pace, which can be reassuring, especially if you're starting out on your investment journey.

The Adventure of Mutual Funds: Your Investment Club

Imagine a mutual fund as a treasure chest, not filled with gold and jewels, but with a mix of exciting investments like stocks, bonds, and sometimes real estate. Managed by expert fund managers, this chest is constantly curated to ensure its contents remain valuable.

Think of investing in a mutual fund as joining an exclusive club. Each member contributes money, pooling resources to buy a diverse range of investments. This approach allows for purchasing more varied assets than what one could afford individually, making it perfect for young adventurers like you, Benjamin, who are just starting their investment journey.

The strength of mutual funds lies in their diversity, hunting to a treasure chest being more thrilling when filled with different types of jewels. This diversification means that if one investment in the fund falters, others can balance it out, keeping your investment safe and growing. It's like exploring various paths in a treasure hunt - if one is blocked, others are available.

Choosing mutual funds is a wise decision for several reasons. They are accessible, even with modest amounts of money, and offer the advantage of professional management. By investing in a mutual fund, you essentially own a portion of a vast array of investments, which can collectively contribute to the growth of your wealth over time.

Options: Like a Coupon for Stocks!

Understanding Options: A Peek into a Complex World

In our journey through the finance world, there's an investment type called options. They're a ticket to a future event, but instead of a concert or sports game, it's a chance to buy or sell something at a set price.

What Are Options?

Imagine you have a coupon that lets you buy your favorite ice cream at a special price before the end of the month. Options are similar. They give you the right to buy or sell a certain amount of something (like stocks or commodities) at a specific price. This is known as the 'strike price,' and you must decide by a particular date, called the' expiration date.' (5)

For example, you can buy shares in a company at $10 each, and you have until the end of December to decide. If the company's stock price goes up to $15, you can still buy it at $10 because of your option. But if the price falls below $10, you might choose not to buy it.

Why Are Options Complex?

Options are pretty complex and not typically used by individual investors, especially young ones. They are like a complicated puzzle requiring much knowledge and quick thinking. Trading options means you must look at many factors and be ready to change your plans quickly based on the market's moves. (6)
Options trading can be expensive and risky. It's like playing a challenging video game where you need to make many quick decisions, and there's a risk of losing. That's why options are usually left to professional traders with much experience.

In the big world of investing, options are one of the more complex paths. They offer unique opportunities but also come with their own set of challenges and risks.

Attention Parents: Mid-Book Review Request

Be a Super Review Hero!

Your Review Can Change the World!

"Sharing is caring, and caring makes the world go 'round!" - A Wise Kid

Hey awesome readers! Did you know that when you share something good, like a helpful book, you make the world a little bit brighter? It's true! Just like superheroes use their powers to save the day, you can use your superpower of sharing to help other kids learn about money and business. How cool is that?

I've got a super mission for you. Imagine you have the power to help a kid just like you - someone curious, full of dreams, and ready to learn about the big, exciting world of the stock market!

Our book, ***The Financially Savvy Kid's Guide: a Mini Mogul's Introduction to the Stock Market,*** is like a treasure map to understanding money, companies, and how the stock market works. But to share this treasure with more kids, we need your superhero help.

Here's the plan: We need your superpower of writing a review for this book. Why? Because just like you pick a new game or toy based on what others say, other kids and their parents choose books based on reviews. Your words could open up a whole new world for another kid!

Think about it – your review could help!

Another kid starts their own money-making adventure.

A future young entrepreneur learns the secrets of business.

Someone just like you discover the fun in finance.

A dreamer believes they can be a stock market superstar too!

The Financially Savvy Kid's Guide

Ready to be a hero? Just scan the QR code below to zap over to the review page:

If you're excited about helping a fellow young adventurer, then you're a true super reviewer! Welcome to the team of change-makers and dream-believers!

I can't wait to show you more amazing money secrets and stock market tips in the next chapters of our adventure. Together, we'll make learning about finance super fun!

Thank you from the bottom of my superhero heart for your support and for being a part of this incredible journey.

Your biggest fan and fellow adventurer, Savvy Books Publishing

P.S. - Remember, every time you help someone by sharing something valuable, you become their hero! If you think this book could be a treasure map for another young explorer, share it with them. *Let's spread the fun and knowledge!*

Economics and Economies

How the Worlds shares resources

Exploring Domestic and World Economies:

The Big Cookie Jar:

Let's embark on a fun adventure to understand how economies work. Imagine your favorite jar full of cookies. Some cookies you made yourself, some your friends gave you, and others you bought from the store. You can enjoy these cookies, share them with others, or even trade them for a cool toy. This is like an economy

– all about making, sharing, and using things. (2)

Domestic vs. World Economies

Your home, where you and your family make and use things, is like a "domestic" economy. It's all about how you and your family manage what you have. But when we talk about the "world" economy, think of it as a vast global cookie jar where everyone's making, buying, and selling things – not just cookies, but all sorts of goods and services, all over the planet. (3)

How Economies Grow

Economies grow and change just like you do. They start small and simple, like a seed, and then grow bigger and more complex. At first, people might only make things they really need, like food and shelter. Economists call this a "traditional economy".(3) But as people learn new skills and create new tools, they start making more varied things, like clothes, toys, and, yes, even cookies! This growth and change is called "economic development." (4)

Why Economies Matter to Us

Economies are super important in our daily lives. They influence what we eat, where we live, how we learn, and the ways we have fun. (1) For example, when you buy a toy, you're a part of the economy. Your money helps the store, the toy maker, and even those who make toy materials. This cycle of buying and selling keeps the economy moving and allows people to have jobs and earn money. (4)

Economies also help us make choices. Imagine you have $5. You could buy a book or a toy or save it for something later. Making such decisions is what economists call "economic decisions." (2)

So, remember, an economy isn't just about money; it's about how we all live, work, and play together. And just like the cookies in a jar and benefit, we all contribute to form the economy.

The World Economies and the Stock Market: A Global Game of Business

Imagine the world as a giant playground where every country has a unique game involving making and selling things. These games are like different economies. Imagine a scoreboard showing how well each game is going, with points based on how much they're making and selling. This scoreboard is like the stock market.

How World Economies Connect to the Stock Market

Each country's economy is like a team in this global game. The different areas in the world make products, like toys and clothes, or provide services, like teaching and healthcare. When these economies do well, their companies usually make more money. This success then shows up on the stock market, where people buy and sell shares of these companies.

For example, let's say a country is really good at making video games and selling them worldwide. Companies that make these games may become more valuable. People who invest in the stock market see this and might want to buy shares in those gaming companies. When lots of people want to buy shares, the price of those shares usually goes up. This is how good things happening in the world economies can lead to higher stock prices.

The Stock Market as a Reflection

The stock market is like a big mirror that reflects what's happening in world economies. Suppose economies are strong and making many things people want to buy. In that case, the stock market usually looks good – stock prices go up, and investors are happy. But if economies are having a tough time, maybe because fewer people are buying things or there are problems in the world, the stock market can reflect that, too, with lower stock prices.

This connection between world economies and the stock market is important because it helps people decide where to invest their money. It's like choosing which game on the playground looks the most fun or has the best chance of winning.

So, the stock market and world economies are closely linked. They tell us a lot about how countries and companies are doing in this big, exciting worldwide game of business.

Chapter 4: Putting your new Knowledge to Work!

The Young Investor: A Guide to Growing Your Money Tree

Welcome to the last chapter of our adventure in stock investing! You've learned a lot, and now it's time to look at how you can start your journey as a young investor.

The Importance of Starting Early

Why start investing early? Just like a tree needs time to grow from a tiny seed into a magnificent giant, your investments also need time to grow. The sooner you start, the more time your money has to blossom. (1)

The Magic of Compounding

Albert Einstein famously said, "Compound interest is the eighth wonder of the world. He who understands it earns it; he who doesn't pays it." (1) Imagine putting money in a special account. The bank gives you extra money, called interest, as a 'thank you.' The magic is in the compounding - you earn interest not just on your original money but also on the interest you've already gained! Your money grows like a snowball rolling down a hill, getting bigger and bigger. (1)

Investing for Future Purchases

Investing can be a smart way to afford expensive things. Say you want a new video game. Instead of spending your money immediately, you could invest it. Over time, this money might grow enough to buy the game with some to spare! This teaches patience and the value of waiting. (2)

How to Find Stock Information and Read a Ticker Tape

Now, how do you find information about stocks? You can look at a ticker tape, like a moving belt of information you see on financial news channels or websites. It shows stock symbols (abbreviations for company names) and numbers that tell you how the stock is doing. For example, 'AAPL 143.50 ↑ 2.05' means Apple's stock is currently priced at $143.50, up $2.05 from before. (2)

Understanding Financial Statements

Financial statements are like report cards for companies. They tell you how much money a company made, spent, and saved. You can find them on business news websites or a company's website under their 'Investor Relations' section. These statements can be complex, but they'll help you understand a company's health as you learn more. (2)

Remember, investing is powerful but comes with risks. Always talk to a trusted adult if you need more time to invest money you can afford to lose. (1)

Real Kids, Real Money, and Real Life: We learned this, but let's review!

Investing is for everyone, even kids:

You don't have to be a grown-up to start learning about investing. With help from adults, like parents or teachers, you can begin to understand how investing works. Think of it as planting a seed. That seed can grow into a strong tree with care and patience, just like your investments can grow over time.

The stock market is like a big, global game:

The stock market is constantly moving, with prices going up and down. It's like a giant game where companies are the players, and their stocks are the scores. These scores change based on how well the company is doing. If a company is doing great, its stock value might go up. But the value might go down if it needs to do better. It's a game that requires strategy, patience, and a bit of luck!

Understanding 'Securities': More than Just Stocks

Exploring the World Beyond Stocks: The Amazing World of Securities!

What are Securities?

Think of securities like a treasure chest full of different jewels. Each jewel is a different type of investment. Stocks are like sparkling diamonds, but there are other gems, too! These are common securities besides stocks:

- **Bonds**: Bonds are like getting a promise note from a friend. When you buy a bond, a company or the government promises to pay you back the money you lent them, with a little extra as a 'thank you' (like interest). It's like lending money to a friend who promises to give it back with an extra candy!
- **Mutual Funds**: Now, imagine a big box filled with different kinds of candies - that's a mutual fund. It's a mix of various investments like stocks, bonds, and others managed by experts. It's a great way to have a variety of assets all in one place.

Why Diverse Investments Matter

Why not just stick with one type of investment, like stocks? Well, having a mix of different investments is like having different kinds of treasure chest, like gems , like candies ,like tools in your toolbox. If one tool doesn't work for a job, another will!

- **Spreading the Risk**: If you only have stocks and they go down in value, you might lose money. But if you have bonds and mutual funds, they might do well even if stocks don't. It's like not putting all your eggs in one basket.
- **Balanced Growth**: Different investments grow in different ways. You can balance the risks and chances of growth by having a variety. It's like having a garden with different kinds of plants, each growing in its own way.

So, there you have it! Securities are more than just stocks. They're a whole world of exciting opportunities waiting for you to explore. Remember, investing is not just about making money; it's about making intelligent choices. And who knows? Maybe one day, you'll become a master of the investment world, thanks to your knowledge of securities!

The Role of the Economy in the Stock Market

"The Big Picture: How the World Economy Plays a Game with Stocks!"

"Hey there, young adventurers! Ready to understand how the big, wide world affects the stock market? It's like a giant puzzle where each piece affects the other. Today, we will explore how the global economy and stocks are connected.

Global Economy and Stocks

Imagine the world as a massive network of countries, each doing different things like making products, providing services, and trading with each other. This big network is called the global economy. Now, think of stock prices like balloons in the air. When the global economy is strong and happy, these balloons float higher, meaning stock prices go up! But when the economy faces trouble, like a big storm, the balloons might start to sink lower, and stock prices can drop.

- **Watching the World**: Keeping an eye on global events is like being a detective with a magnifying glass. If a significant event happens in one part of the world, it can affect stock prices. For example, if there's a new invention in one country, it might increase stock in technology companies.

Economic Indicators: Clues to the Economy's Health

Like how doctors use thermometers to check your temperature, economists use 'economic indicators' to check the economy's health. These indicators are clues that tell us how things are going.

- **Unemployment Rates**: This tells us how many people have jobs. When many people work, they can buy things, which is good for businesses and their stocks. But if many people need jobs, they might only spend a little, which can be challenging for businesses and their stocks.
- **Consumer Spending**: This is all about how much money people are spending. If people are buying lots of stuff, it usually means they're confident about the economy, and this can boost stock prices.

So, for young investors, understanding the economy is like having a map while exploring a treasure island. It helps you see where you're going and make smart choices on your investment journey. The world economy is a big, exciting puzzle, and now you know how it fits with the stock market. Keep exploring, keep learning, and who knows? You might just become a master navigator of the stock market seas!

Smart Steps for Safe Investing: Your Guide to Being a Wise Young Investor!

Hey there, future finance wizards! Ready to learn about safe investing? Think of it like learning to ride a bike. You start with training wheels and take small, careful rides before you zoom off on big adventures. That's just like intelligent investing!

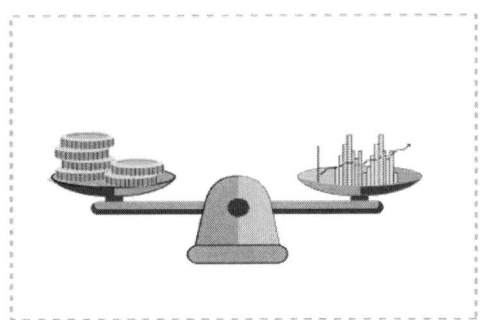

Start Small and Learn

Imagine you're building a tower with blocks. You wouldn't start with the biggest block, right? You'd start small and steady. That's how you should think about investing, too.

- **Baby Steps**: Just like you learn a new game step by step, start your investing journey with small, manageable investments. It's like planting a tiny seed and watching it grow.
- **Learn as You Grow**: Each small investment is a learning opportunity. You'll understand more about how stocks work and feel more confident as you go along. It's like leveling up in a game – the more you play, the better you get!

The Importance of Research

Before you pick a stock, become a detective! Research is key. It's like choosing your team in a game based on who's the strongest and most intelligent.

- **Company Homework**: Look into the companies behind the stocks. What do they do? Are they successful? It's like checking a character's stats in a video game before you choose them.
- **Understanding the Market**: Just like reading the rules before playing a game, understand how the stock market works. The more you know, the better choices you can make.

So, young explorers, as you step into the world of investing, remember to start small, do your research, and learn from others. Safe investing is about being intelligent, patient, and curious. Keep these tips in your adventurer's backpack, and you're sure to find success on your financial journey. Who knows, you may become the next famous young investor!

Adventure Awaits!

Remember, this book is like the first chapter of a thrilling adventure novel. The investing world is vast and full of mysteries to solve, treasures to find, and exciting paths to explore. You've started on a path that's both fun and full of learning opportunities.

Stay Curious and Keep Learning

Like a detective never stops looking for clues, don't stop asking questions. The more curious you are, the more you'll discover. Each question you request and every little bit you learn adds another sparkling coin to your treasure chest of knowledge.

Building Your Future

Every page you read and understand in this book has laid a brick on your path to becoming a savvy investor. This path doesn't end here; it's just the beginning! The more you read and learn, the stronger and more fantastic your financial future becomes.

The World of the Stock Market Awaits!

So, what's next, future mini moguls? Are you ready to dive deeper into the world of investing? The stock market is an ever-changing, exciting landscape waiting for young explorers like you to make their mark.

A Big Cheer for You!

You've shown incredible focus and dedication by completing this book. That's no small feat! You're already showing the makings of a great investor – patience, curiosity, and the drive to learn.

As you close this book, remember that your adventure in finance is just starting. Keep reading, exploring, and, most importantly, having fun! The stock market world is waiting for you, and who knows what amazing things you'll discover next! Congratulations once again, and happy investing, future mini moguls! The sky's the limit! "

Your Amazing Journey in Financial Literacy: A Lifelong Adventure!

"Embarking on a Lifetime of Learning, Creativity, and Smart Investing!"

As we end our exciting journey through the world of stocks and investments, I want to share some vital wisdom with you. This isn't just the end of a book; it's the beginning of a lifelong adventure in financial literacy. Think of it as an epic quest in a vast, ever-changing world where you're the hero, learning and growing with every step.

Financial Literacy

Imagine you're the captain of a ship on a vast ocean. The world of finance is that ocean – vast, deep, and full of wonders. Just like the ocean, it keeps changing and revealing new secrets. Financial literacy isn't something you learn once; it's a continuous journey. Money and investing evolve daily, and there's always something new to discover.

- **Keep Learning**: Like how you level up in video games, your financial knowledge grows every time you learn something new. This could be a new word, like 'dividend,' or understanding why a company's stock price went up or down.
- **Stay Updated**: The world of finance is always buzzing with news – companies launching new products, governments making new policies or even new technologies changing how we use money.

Creativity and Knowledge: Your Superpowers

As an investor, you've got two superpowers: creativity and knowledge. Let's explore how these powers can help you on your financial quest.

- **Creativity**: This is your ability to think outside the box. Investing is about imagining the possibilities – which companies will grow, what new

inventions could change the world, and how you can be part of that growth.
- **Knowledge**: This is what you know and understand about finance. The more you know, the better decisions you can make. It's like having a map and a compass on your adventure.

Investing: A Team Effort with Your Parents

Now, a word of caution. Investing can be fun and rewarding, but it's also serious business. It involves real money and real risks. That's why involving your parents or guardians in your investment journey are super important.

- **Ask for Guidance**: Your parents can help you understand the risks and benefits of investing. They can also guide you in setting up a savings or even a small investment account if they think you're ready.
- **Learn Together**: Your parents are learning about investing, too. This can be

an excellent opportunity for you to learn together. You can discuss news, share ideas, and make investment decisions as a team.

Looking Ahead: Your Bright Future

So, what does the future hold for you, young investor? The possibilities are endless! You may become a savvy stock market player, an entrepreneur with a brilliant business idea, or a wise saver planning for a bright future. Whatever path you choose, remember these key things:

- **Stay Curious**: Always ask questions and seek answers. The world is full of fantastic learning opportunities.
- **Be Patient**: Good things take time. Just like a tree doesn't grow overnight, your financial knowledge and investments will grow over time.
- **Have Fun**: Enjoy the journey! Learning about money and investing can be fun if

you approach it enthusiastically and positively.

And finally, remember, you're not alone on this journey. You've got your family, friends, teachers, and many others who are cheering you on. Keep your spirit of adventure alive, and embrace the exciting world of financial literacy with open arms.

Congratulations on taking the first steps on this incredible journey. I can't wait to see where it takes you. Happy learning and investing, and here's to your bright, successful future!

A Final Note to Parents: Nurturing Financial Literacy in Your Child

Dear Parents,
As you and your child reach the end of "The Financially Savvy Kid's Guide," I want to extend my heartfelt congratulations and share

some important insights with you. Financial literacy is not just a skill; it's a vital life lesson, as crucial as any subject your child learns in school or at home. Yet, it's often one of the most overlooked areas in a child's education. This guide is just the beginning of a rewarding journey for you and your child.

The Importance of Financial Literacy

Understanding money management, investments, savings, and the economy is as essential as learning to read, write, or ride a bike. It prepares your child for the real world, equipping them with the tools to make informed decisions, avoid debt, and achieve financial stability. Studies have shown that children taught about finances early are more likely to be successful and less stressed about money as adults. (3)

Starting Conversations Early

It's never too early to start talking about money with your child. The concepts in this book are designed to spark curiosity and initiate meaningful conversations. By discussing topics like saving, investing, and the value of money, you're laying a solid foundation for their financial understanding and habits.

Learning Together

As you guide your child through their financial education, remember that this is a learning journey for both of you. Reading further on these subjects, perhaps in more advanced texts or through online resources, can enhance your understanding and provide more context to the discussions with your child. Engaging in this together strengthens your bond and reinforces the learning process for both of you.

Patience is Key

The world of finance can sometimes be complex and overwhelming. It's essential to be patient with yourself and your child as you navigate these new concepts. Remember, learning about finance is a gradual process. If a topic seems challenging, take a step back, review it, or find alternative sources that explain it differently. The goal is to build a solid and positive understanding of financial matters; take your time with them.

Perseverance Matters

There will be moments when a particular financial concept might seem too complicated or abstract. In these moments, your perseverance as a parent and a teacher becomes most crucial. Encouraging your child to keep going, even when challenging, instills a sense of resilience and determination. These qualities will help them succeed in understanding finances and all areas of life.

A Note of Thanks

Lastly, thank you for reading "The Financially Savvy Kid's Guide" with your child. By doing so, you're actively preparing them for a financially responsible and informed future. Your involvement and interest in their financial education is a priceless gift that will benefit them throughout their life.

Remember, financial literacy is a journey, not a destination. Each step, no matter how small, is progress towards empowering your child with the knowledge and skills they will use for a lifetime.

With warm regards and best wishes on your continued journey,

Keeping the Game Alive

Wow, you did it! You've zoomed through the pages, explored the twists and turns of the stock market, and discovered the secrets of financial literacy. You're now a mini mogul in training! But guess what? The adventure doesn't end here. Now, it's your turn to pass the baton and guide others on this thrilling journey.

Think of your favorite video game. When you find a cool trick or hidden level, don't you just want to share it with your friends? That's exactly what you can do with the knowledge you've gained from our book! By sharing your honest thoughts about The Financially Savvy Kid's Guide: A Mini Mogul's Introduction to the Stock Market on Amazon, you're pointing other kids and parents towards the treasure of financial wisdom. Your review is like a secret code that unlocks the world of finance for others. It's a beacon, shining brightly to guide future mini moguls to the knowledge they're seeking. And guess what? Your words have the power to inspire a passion for financial literacy, business, and entrepreneurship in others.

We can't thank you enough for your help. Remember, children's financial literacy isn't just a single game – it's a never-ending quest. And by passing on what you've learned, you're keeping the game alive, exciting, and accessible for everyone.

Are you ready to be a hero again? Click the link below and share your thoughts. It's your time to shine!

Click here to leave your review on Amazon.

Every review counts, and yours is the key to unlocking a world of financial savvy for others. So thank you for being awesome, for sharing your journey, and for helping to spread the magic of financial literacy. Keep shining, young mogul!

The Grand Finale: Celebrating Your Journey into the World of Investing!

"Hip Hip Hooray! You're on Your Way to Being a Mini Mogul!"

"Wow! Give yourself a big round of applause! You've just crossed the finish line of 'The Financially Savvy Kid's Guide: A Mini Mogul's Introduction to the Stock Market.' You're not just any reader; you're a future financial whiz who's taken an incredible journey into the world of stocks, bonds, and smart investing!

References:

Chapter 1

Section 1

1. Investopedia. (2023). Stock Definition. Retrieved from Investopedia website.
2. Corporate Finance Institute. (2023). What is a Company? Retrieved from Corporate Finance Institute website.
3. Investopedia. (2023). Public Company Definition. Retrieved from Investopedia website.
4. Corporate Finance Institute. (2023). Private Company Definition. Retrieved from Corporate Finance Institute website.
5. Investopedia. (2023). Stock Definition. Retrieved from Investopedia website.
6. Corporate Finance Institute. (2023). Company Definition. Retrieved from Corporate Finance Institute website.

7. *Investopedia. (2023). Public Company vs. Private Company. Retrieved from Investopedia website.*

Section 2

1. *Smith, J. (2023). A history of stock markets. New York: ABC Publishing.*
2. *CNBC. (2023). S&P 500, Nasdaq finish higher to clinch longest winning streaks since November 2021: Live updates. Retrieved from https://www.cnbc.com/live-blog/stock-market-live-today/*
3. *Toyota Motor Corporation. (n.d.). Retrieved from https://www.toyota.com/*
4. *Sony Corporation. (n.d.). Retrieved from https://www.sony.com/*
5. *Nintendo Co., Ltd. (n.d.). Retrieved from https://www.nintendo.com/*
6. *The Balance. (2021). The Origins of Bull and Bear Markets. https://www.thebalance.*
7. *https://www.fidelity.com/trading/investing-in-ipos*

Chapter 2:

Section 1:

1. *Investopedia. (n.d.). Benjamin Graham. Retrieved from <https://www.investopedia.com/terms/b/>*
2. *Wikipedia. (2023, December 8). Benjamin Graham. Retrieved from Wikipedia.*
3. *Wikipedia. (2023, November 27). Warren Buffett. Retrieved from Wikipedia.*
4. *Wikipedia. (2023, November 27). Bill Ackman. Retrieved from Wikipedia.*
5. *Wikipedia. (2023, November 29). Carl Icahn. Retrieved from Wikipedia.*
6. *Richard, C. S. (2010). Confidence Game: How Hedge Fund Manager Bill Ackman Called Wall Street's Bluff. Wiley.*
7. *Stevens, M. (1993). King Icahn: The Biography of a Renegade Capitalist. Dutton Adult.*

Section 2:

1. *Graham, B. (2006). The Intelligent Investor. Harper Business.*

2. Khan, M. Y. (2013). *Financial Services*. Tata McGraw-Hill Education.
3. Murphy, J. J. (1999). *Technical Analysis of the Financial Markets*. New York Institute of Finance.
4. Dreman, D. (1998). *Contrarian Investment Strategies: The Psychological Edge*. Free Press.
5. Bodie, Z., Kane, A., & Marcus, A. J. (2018). *Investments*. McGraw-Hill Education.
6. Financial Industry Regulatory Authority. (2020). *Day-Trading: Your Dollars at Risk*. FINRA.org.
7. Investor.gov. (n.d.). *Day Trading*. Investor.gov.
8. Securities and Exchange Commission. (2020). *Day Trading*. SEC.gov.
9. Hagstrom, R. G. (2013). *The Warren Buffett Way*. Wiley.

Chapter 3

Section 1:

1. *Investopedia. (2021). What Is an Index Fund?Investopedia.com.*
2. *Buffett, W., & Clark, D. (2008). Warren Buffett's Management Secrets: Proven Tools for Personal and Business Success. Simon & Schuster.*
3. *Investopedia. (2021). What Is a Bond Fund?Investopedia.com.*
4. *Morningstar. (2021). Bond Funds. Morningstar.com.*
5. *U.S. Securities and Exchange Commission. (2020). Investor.gov - Bond Funds. Investor.gov.*
6. *Investopedia. (2021). What Are Options?Investopedia.com.*
7. *Chicago Board Options Exchange. (2020). Understanding Options Trading. CBOE.com.*

Section 2:

1. *Samuelson, P. A., & Nordhaus, W. D. (2010). Economics. McGraw-Hill Education.*
2. *Mankiw, N. G. (2014). Principles of Economics. Cengage Learning.*

3. *Todaro, M. P., & Smith, S. C. (2011). Economic Development. Pearson.*

4. *Sachs, J. D., & Larrain, F. B. (1993). Macroeconomics in the Global Economy. Prentice Hall.*

5. *Krugman, P., & Wells, R. (2009). Economics. Worth Publishers.*

Section 3:

1. *Bodie, Z., Kane, A., & Marcus, A. J. (2018). Investments. McGraw-Hill Education.*

2. *Kobliner, B. (2020). Make Your Kid a Money Genius (Even If You're Not). Simon & Schuster.*

3. *Sullivan, R., Anderson, S. G., & Harris, M. (2017). Personal Financial Planning for Executives and Entrepreneurs: The Path to Financial Peace of Mind. Palgrave Macmillan.*

Fun Facts Reference List:

1. *Deepthi Nair. (2021, August 17). How teenage traders are turning their pocket*

money into profits. The National. Retrieved from <https://www.thenationalnews.com>

2. *Deepthi Nair. (2021, August 17). How teenage traders are turning their pocket money into profits. The National. Retrieved from <https://www.thenationalnews.com>*

3. *Consumer Financial Protection Bureau. (2020). The importance of financial literacy for kids. Retrieved from [CFPB website]*

Savvy Books Publishing

Printed in Great Britain
by Amazon